Letters from Lauren

Letters from Lauren

A Journey of Self-Discovery, Awareness, & Growth

LAUREN DARLINGTON

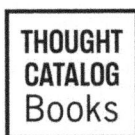

THOUGHT
CATALOG
Books

BROOKLYN, NY

THOUGHT
CATALOG
Books

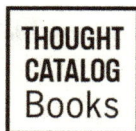

Published by Thought Catalog Books, a division of The Thought & Expression Co.,
Williamsburg, Brooklyn. Founded in 2010, Thought Catalog is a website and
imprint dedicated to your ideas and stories. We publish fiction and non-fiction
from emerging and established writers across all genres. For general information
and submissions: manuscripts@thoughtcatalog.com.

First edition, 2017

ISBN: 978-1945796494

Printed and bound in the United States.

10 9 8 7 6 5 4 3 2 1

A journey of self-discovery, awareness, and growth.

I am here to embrace all that was,
evolve into all I am, and
empower others to do the same.

Contents

Part III. Empower

Introduction

Finding words to share my journey has always been a love of mine. I find myself delving deep into my soul and sharing what comes up in hope that others know they are never alone. *Letters from Lauren* was birthed from this space. A space of vulnerability, of wanting to share my lessons, and of wanting to empower others to live their lives with curiosity and freedom from the limits they place on themselves.

In the pages to come, I will share snippets of my young life. My wish is that through the words to follow, you will find hope in times of need, comfort in times of loneliness, empowerment in times of struggle, and, above all, the realisation that no matter what your life was, you hold the power to make it what it will become. I aim to evoke a curiosity within you, a desire to question your world more.

Before reading these letters, I wanted to provide you with some insight into who I am. Why listen to me? Why read this without first knowing who I am and where I have come from?

I was once a slave to my own mind, completely consumed by thoughts within. I tried medication, therapy, self-destructive behaviours, being positive, and suppression but nothing worked. I spent years battling a mental health diagnosis. I endured countless visits to hospitals, suicide attempts, lost a loved one to suicide, lost relationships, gained others, and experienced abuse. Like everyone, I had my own battles to overcome. I resigned to the fact that I was a victim and that was my life, yet I failed to see that I was labeling myself, putting myself in a box I would later find I could destroy. I have now come to a place where I see myself and, in turn, my world differently. I no longer label myself as a diagnosis or chase a world of positivity. I no longer take medication or see therapists; I no longer engage in self-destructive behaviour or see myself as a victim of my life. I am in a space of awareness, curiosity, and constant growth, and it is a space I want to share with others.

I like to sign my work with 'unapologetically yours' because I am tired of reading apologies for our voices. Whether we shrink, hide, or adjust our voices, we are altering our words and ideas to fit the world around us. And it is enough. So I sign off 'unapologetically yours' because I won't apologise for my voice nor should you. My words are simply my thoughts and observations—*mine*. I do not claim to know everything or even be correct, but I do know that my words are real and honest and ones that I will not hide.

I am not a psychologist. I am not a doctor. I am not a specialist in any given field—but I am a girl who has fought battles and feels a need to share them with the world. There is nothing superior about me or what I have done; there is no luck I have experienced that separates you from me; there is no special quality I have that you don't. I am just a girl with some words to share. So please, know that everything you need you have within you, your life, and your world right now.

PART 1

Embrace

*I embrace everything in my life,
for I now see the purpose it all serves.*

Self-Destruction

You latched onto my skin
Stripping me of my purity
Marking me forever
Leaving a crimson trail of my demons
For all to see

I stop for a moment and look down, my arm decorated before me. My demons clear for all to see, patterns of crimson lines my arm. A wave of calm washes over me; I can breathe, my mind blank. I feel nothing. I close my eyes and allow the nothingness to engulf me, but it escapes my body as quickly as it came. Rushing away, fast. Leaving behind a fire in its place. My arm burns, my heart races, and my stomach turns. What have I done?

It started as nothing; it was barely a scratch, barely a visible line, but my nothing screamed volumes. I stared at my once-blank and beautifully innocent arm now with lines of red, illustrating a story. One I was too ashamed to tell. I watch as the lines before me paint the song I repeated in my head every day—I wasn't enough, never enough. And now, everyone could see how not enough I was.

I didn't know what else to do; the thoughts in my mind became too heavy, too painful to carry on my own. I crumbled under the weight of them and could no longer bear their load. I had to find a release, to find some silence, if only fleeting. I needed a break. And this is what it became—a break; a fleeting moment of peace; physical pain to express my internal struggle—I needed something.

And I wished so badly it would stay this way, that a few scratches, a few painted lines, would suffice. I fooled myself into thinking it would, it would remain harmless, simply a quiet cry for help.

Yet self-harm became so much more.

What followed was years of addiction, years of coming back

for more. Whenever I would try to escape, her seductive dance would recommence, always pulling me back for more. She pushed back in whenever I tried to fight, knocking on my doors whenever I kicked her out, and always persevering for more.

Self-harm took over my life; we became one, unable to leave without a release nearby. Soon she was seeping into my veins and becoming who I was, acting like a fog over my view, a haze covering the world, covering who I was. Self-harm became my every thought, my daily routine, and my all-consuming addiction. She was my undoing; she had sucked me in and I couldn't bear to lose her. She was the perfect trap, self-destruction and reliance in one dangerous package.

But self-harm didn't win. She tried, and time and time again my body wore the proof. My skin decorated with lines, letters, and shapes I would carry for life, my pain forever etched into my skin. But she never won. Each time I felt more helpless, more stuck, and more certain that this would be it—but it never was. And for what reason I never knew, but looking back I can see I was never meant to leave. Self-harm was my past; she served a purpose I needed, lessons I had to endure, pain I needed to feel. She is a part of my story but only a mere chapter in the life of me.

I was never meant to leave, though I would falter again.

Unapologetically yours,

Lauren

2

10 Things Anyone Recovering from Self-Harm Needs to Know

1. It isn't going to be easy. Recovering from anything isn't. Like an alcoholic craving one more drop of liquid gold, we will crave the rush from our addiction again, too. We will feel like we have recovered, finally free, but relapses will sneak in. If one knocks on your door, don't feel the weight of failure consuming you. Instead, ask her why she's here; get to know who invited her. Being curious brings awareness, and through awareness, you can prevent future visits.

2. We will try multiple things before finding what works. I'm sorry, but it is highly unlikely that the first thing we try will be a success. And there may not be one single thing. Don't give up if you take time to work it out.

3. It will be uncomfortable. I wish I could lie and say it is as simple as just stopping. But it isn't. Nothing is. Like that afternoon chocolate craving that rises daily, self-harm is a hard addiction to curb. It will bring up emotions, feelings, and thoughts you silenced for so long. But know that you can't just suppress this forever.

4. We may outgrow people or situations. It's life. Who we spend time with now may not be the same in five years. And a change of season in life can expedite this process. We may no longer connect with the same people. And that's okay.

5. Medication isn't the answer. We don't need a pill to 'fix' us. We aren't broken. Please, please don't look for an external fix for an internal battle.

6. Be patient. We all likely didn't develop our relationship with self-harm over night, so don't expect her to leave the morning after. It will take time. It will be hard. Be patient.

7. Other demons may surface. We used self-harm to suppress something we didn't want to feel or face. So when you evict her from your life, new demons will likely apply to take her place. You may find you feel worse before you feel better. Know that you can overcome this too.

8. Don't replace one addiction with another. But please don't replace self-harm with one of her family members. Her sister, smoking, may seem like a good idea, but she just brings her own baggage we will need to untangle later.

9. It is worth the effort. You are probably reading this and wanting to quit already, but know that it is worth the effort. Those nights we feel completely worthless and alone…those days we swear you can't go on…they are specks in the span of our life. They are behind us, and by overcoming them now, you have your life ahead to create the world you wish. Overcoming something as difficult as this builds strength in us that we will carry on in life. So please know, it is worth it.

10. We will be okay. Regardless of how many times we may fall; how many relapses may surface; how uncomfortable we may feel—we will be okay. There is nothing that is too much for us, I promise you that. Emotions pass. And this will to.

Unapologetically yours,

Lauren

3

Labels, Pills, and Justifications

There is safety in it;
A diagnosis.
One word to define myself by
A word to explain it all
A label I would cling to
Justification for all I lacked

We are so quick to attach ourselves to a label, a diagnosis, a justification for 'why we are the way we are.' So eager to find an explanation, a comforting word to bring reassurance that we are, in fact, 'sick.' Constantly googling symptoms, self-diagnosing behaviours, and seeking medical approval to confirm that there is something wrong with us. Being sick starts to feel…safe. Like we need an external justification for all the turmoil we feel inside.

We avoid the voice that's sitting in our stomach, weighing heavy on our daily world. We know this voice is ours and that she's saying that something isn't right. But she is too hard to hear, too confronting to face, so instead, we seek help—a label will fix us all.

And so we get it: our first diagnosis. Medication to numb the symptoms, to hide them, to band-aid them, soon follows. At first it works; we find the solitude we sought, the numbness we need, and the suppression that's comfortable. Yet over time, we need more. We need a stronger pill, more prescriptions, and higher doses. Because the nagging voice within, the voice that is screaming something isn't right—gets louder. Her voice begins to pierce our ears in the early hours of the morning and sits heavy on our chests late at night and tugs at our silence in moments of rest.

So the cycle continues. Diagnosis, pills, new diagnosis, more pills. All the while we are pushing the voice we need to hear further and further down, suffocating her day in and day out.

We become addicted to the cycle, the harsh reality of those words feels uncomfortable to say—but it's my truth. I thrived on being sick, I could do it so well. Diagnosis I sought, symptoms I justified, labels I held on to. I could do sick, I was loved sick, I was comforted sick, and I knew sick.

I was on a never-ending chase for a reason, constantly asking 'why?' I was asking the right questions at the time but seeking the answers in the wrong places. I was searching for a label, an excuse to behave this way. My 'why' was my desire to understand myself more, but at the time the answers I desired—I needed—were ones to keep me stuck. My 'why' was to find comfort and safety; my 'why' was to hide.

My diagnosis became my explanation; it was my reason for all my pain and dysfunction. It explained in one word that there was something wrong with my wiring and my reactions in life weren't my fault, they were the fault of my mental illness. There was safety in this; I could hide, and I did it well.

I hid under avoidance, medication, therapy, blame, guilt, suppression—whatever form I could run with, I did.

I hid for months, determined that I could run forever. But the more I pushed, the further away I ran, the louder the voice became. Time after time I fell, again and again, unable to carry the weight of my mask anymore. And each time I fell harder and harder until I couldn't get up anymore.

I know now that I was running *into* what I was running away *from*. We are running from not only the cause of our pain but also the solution. In the pain lies our solution, yet we are programmed to turn outwards for peace, for a cure. But I dare to ask: why have we believed for so long that an external fix can heal an internal problem?

We need to stop searching for band-aids and seeking justifications for our emotions and turn inward to see, to ask, to discover what is really going on...

In our pain lies our pleasure.

In our confusion lies our clarity.

In our discomfort lies our answer.

Unapologetically yours,

Lauren

4

Bodies, Shame, and Abandonment

And then I am left.
Empty
Alone
Used

I find myself scrubbing. Scrubbing harder each time the water washes over my body, feeling the warm sensations engulf me—yet my whole body shakes. I feel the bristles scratching harder and harder each time, digging to remove the filth I can't escape. The warmth of the shower no longer leaves a comforting touch. I continue to shake, feeling colder and colder. I find the shower floor and pull my knees in, holding my body tight. I silently close my eyes, bow my head, and scream as hard as I can into my knees, muffling the sound of my voice, once again.

I wonder if I'll ever feel clean. If I can ever erase the taste of the disgust in my mouth. If I will ever escape the flashbacks of the bodies around me. If I will ever let go of the hatred inside—the hatred for everything I now am.

I wonder if I'll ever feel whole. If I can ever see men with love again, if I will ever forgive her for this, if I may ever be touched, held, or kissed again.

I wonder if I'll ever be free. If I am ever let go from the words dancing in my mind. If I am ever able to escape the nightmares that capture me. If I am ever detached from the stories of my past. If I'll ever be able to live without the weight of this secret.

I wonder…

Because I can't live every day like this. I am trapped, a prisoner of my own mind and past, and I want out. I didn't ask for this, did I? And yet I can't find the key to escape. I wake and crave sleep again, the sweet silent nothingness I find with a simple round pill. I crave the escape, the avoidance, and the ignorance it brings.

But I can't escape their bodies. I close my eyes and they're there, suffocating me again and again. I feel the weight of them around me, their hands invading me over and over. I smell the scent in the air, hear their voices in my ear, see the red around me. Each night brings more dreams, more flashbacks, and more nightmares. Every silence brings more words, more degrading whispers, and more abusive remarks. Each morning brings more reality, more fear, and more pain. I just want it to end.

I feel myself slipping more and more into acceptance. This is my life; this is who I am. I begin to accept my fate, those words I've used to define me, the body I see as used. I begin to surrender to the fight; I no longer want to train for war. I begin to lose the fire within me, the spark I know I once had. I begin to give into it all.

Maybe this is all I am worth.

Maybe this is all I am.

Maybe this is all I ever will be...

Unapologetically yours,

Lauren

5

Hi, My Name's Lauren, and I'm an Addict

It's safe
I know the shape of it too well
I can hide
And remain hidden
Always a victim

Looking back I can see now that I was addicted. I was addicted to being a victim. I was addicted to the pride I wore after returning from battle yet again. The praise showered upon me from overcoming my latest relapse became a drug my body craved—a rush I needed to keep myself afloat. But soon it would fade and I would create the same cycle of pain again because I knew that being a victim meant becoming a survivor which brought my sweet, sweet drug back to me again.

I was stuck and I liked being stuck, traveling around on the same merry-go-round. It was safe, it was comfortable, and it was predictable.

I knew after every time I fell I would pick myself up again and be recognised for my resilience. I knew that the validation I so badly craved would come rushing back in. I knew, even if momentarily, that I would feel worthy. I was blinded by the signs that I was craving a constant external fix for something so internally lost.

So I would continue to create situations in which I could play out my lead role. I would relapse, again and again, feeling uncomfortably exhilarated by drama and engaging in conversations I would normally avoid. I was attracting situations to solidify the belief that I was a victim. To affirm this is all I would ever be.

It feels uncomfortable to admit and even more uncomfortable to see the truth, but my cycle is clear now. I see it with fresh eyes and a different lens. I wanted to stay sick because being a victim, staying sick, and being powerless brought the love and attention I wanted. The external love I needed for the lack within. I was seeking external validation for an internal issue, and I was a ticking time bomb.

I embodied my victim mindset, my constant voiceover in my mind reaffirming how terrible my life was—how hard it was to be me, how badly I wanted to be anyone else. I was unable to see through the haze of my mindset and it brought me further and further into the cycle I would continue to play out.

I was stuck. I didn't know what to do, so I stayed stuck.

I stayed in the pattern I knew all too well. And every time I was shown again and again that I was a victim, I fell deeper into my addiction.

What else could I do?

Unapologetically yours,

Lauren

6

Little White Pills and Early Goodbyes

I feel the nothingness wash over me
A wave of calm
This was it
I was done

I watch as my hand fills with white pills of nothingness. One by one popping quicker and quicker as my heart races, my mind blank. I feel my hands shake as they fall. My tears stop, my mind empties, and my heart is heavy. This was it—I couldn't do this anymore. I was done. I closed my eyes, tipped my head back, and one by one the pills danced down my throat. Darkness came fast and heavy; I felt my body go weak, the numbness taking over. I had really done it, I was really leaving.

Everything had become too much to handle. I had pushed away for too long and the harsh reality of everything I was avoiding surfaced for me to see. I couldn't pretend anymore, I couldn't hide anymore, and I couldn't fight anymore. I was so angry, so sad, so lost; I wanted out and I didn't know what else to do.

So I tried. I tried to end it all; I tried to run from everything I couldn't escape. I was done fighting. My pain became too real—suffocating, all-consuming—that the only path I could see was to leave. Say goodbye and slip into a world of nothing.

Yet I know—I can see now—I never fully gave up. Even in the final moments I reached out, I sought help, looking for someone to save me. My best friend was my second chance, changing both our lives forever. A love I never knew why I deserved but always brought me back—every single time. A connection I would hold close to me for eternity. A friendship truly unlike any other. My second chance.

I never knew why; I never understood why I didn't let my future be wiped clean. But I can see now that it wasn't my time.

I never really gave up hope; something in me knew there was more. I just didn't see the way.

I don't know what I believe in—what happens after life, who is above, or if there is an above. I don't know if I feel any certainty about any of it. But I do believe there is someone or something looking out for us all, or maybe there is a life plan we know nothing about. Whatever it is, I'm thankful for it.

Because I know that that wasn't my time to leave; my story wasn't ending there, I had many more chapters to write.

I almost lost everything that day, and it's a time in my life I will never forget. I used to say when you hit rock bottom the only way to go is up, but I think there's more to it than that. I think rock bottom is different for everyone, and you can choose to stay there if you like. I think when you are in moments that feel like the depth of your despair, you have choices to make. At the time, I chose to fight. It was a long, slow, un-strategized fight, but with my army of loved ones, I went to war.

And whilst I would say it was a major milestone in my path, it wasn't the one defining moment that turned me around. Because later I would stumble again, but the fight would continue.

It would continue until I fell into the frustration of it all and stopped rebelling against myself, instead choosing to figure it all out, to find the meaning of my life, to see the crap for what it was—hardship that was painful, heavy, uncomfortable—but serving me.

My early goodbye never came. It wasn't my time. But it did

add another page in my book I call life, another lesson I learnt, another fight that served me.

Unapologetically yours,

Lauren

7

A Letter of Immense Gratitude to my Best Friend

I sometimes feel I dreamt you into life
The friendship I always wanted
A bond I knew I needed
A love like no other

I feel your hand in mine, holding it tight, speaking a thousand words in silence, and I know—I am never alone.

It's the kind of friendship you see in movies. The kind that you always dreamt of as a little girl. The kind of friendship that you just know, with every cell in your body, is forever.

The kind that has overcome struggles, changes, and disagreements. The kind that continued to blossom stronger and stronger each time.

The kind of friendship you can't explain in words. It's a feeling in your soul. The kind you thank the universe for every single day.

The kind of friendship that makes life worth living.

My soulmate.

My forever.

My best friend.

You are my guidance when I'm lost, my reassurance when I'm in doubt, and my love when I'm in pain.

You are my support when times are hard, my calm within my chaos, and my saviour when I'm crumbling.

You are my light in depths of darkness, my forever to my story, my shoulder to my tears.

You are my hand to hold, my phone to call, my mirror to reflect.

You are the other piece of me.

You are my deep belly laughs that hurt my stomach, my inside jokes that no one else finds funny. My crazy teenage memories that we can't believe we survived. You are all of it.

It's the kind of love, the kind of bond that makes no sense but it just works. Our souls belong to one another. Without each other, we wouldn't be us. It's the kind of love our kids will know, our loves share, and the world envies—the kind of love we both needed. I thank the universe every day that we found it.

Thank you for being my future stories, my past memories, and my current reality.

Thank you for being a different kind of love, the kind that compliments companionship without replacing it, that adds to family without detracting from it, and that serves us both in beautiful ways. Thank you for being the kind of love that is like no other—unique and special, its own kind of love.

My soul knows you are its mate, and I am always complete with you.

Thank you for being my light, my love, my guidance, my best friend.

Words will never suffice, but you and I know: our love is worth more than letters.

Unapologetically yours,

Lauren

8

Relapses and Realisations

And when I least expect it,
When I'm no longer searching
There she is

Everything has started to change, yet I still wait for the relapse to sneak in. Feeling my heightened awareness consume my thoughts late at night, waiting for her to pounce when I least expect it again. She always comes back, whatever form she chooses—she always comes back. But this time, she hasn't yet. I wait for her arrival, yet she doesn't turn up. I find myself seeking her out, calling her name, questioning her absence. I know what I'm doing, but it just feels…wrong that she isn't here. Who am I without her visit? Without her labels? Without her pain?

I feel myself crave the return of her, my identity feeling broken. Yet when I hear her footsteps approaching and have a taste of her sweet return, I realise how much has changed.

It starts with mindless eating, my relapse returning in the form of binging. Then as the addiction increases, needing the next hit, I find myself with a swollen stomach once again. But this time I realise, I haven't binged…I just felt like I had.

I ate too much, I was avoiding feeling, I wanted to suppress it all—but I was aware, I wasn't out of control and I realised I was chasing this. I wanted this. I needed this.

It had been months without a taste of it, and I had lost so much of what I once identified myself as, that I needed this reminder—a small taste of what once was. I thought I needed this to feel…me again, but when it came I realised I felt rubbish, truly rubbish, and I remembered why I started on this journey to begin with. And in turn, I became thankful for its return because it showed me that I was different now, how far I had come, how awful it felt.

I realise by expecting my relapse I was welcoming her back in, like sending out an invite to come by she RSVP'd as expected. So not only was I reminded why I wanted her to leave, I was shown to stop asking her back. I had to stop inviting her in.

But this time I saw her in a different light, instead of resenting her visit and self-destructing in the process, I saw the messengers following behind her, the voice I was trying to suppress, the reason behind my need to overeat. This time I saw her with gratitude because through her arrival a spotlight was shone on.

Unapologetically yours,

Lauren

9

An Apology to my Body

It's never enough
I'm never enough
The number decreases, yet I want more
I need more
Will it ever end?

I feel the tenderness of my stomach rub against my shirt, a reminder of what I've just done. I see the wrappers lying around me, mocking me, laughing at my pain. I hear the words thump around in my mind, reminding me over and over of how I had failed. It all becomes too much. The panic rises, the guilt swarms, the weight returns; I have to do something. And then it's clear, calm, obvious. I find the bathroom floor, my fingers gliding down my throat, digging for every last crumb. I rest against the wall—eyes closed and mind silent—even if only for a moment.

You know that body, the one you berate because it won't lose any weight for you?

You know that body, the one you give away because you fail to see its worth?

You know that body, the one you pinch and tug at because you wish so badly to change?

You know that body? It loves you anyway.

We have all spent too long fighting standards that are out of reach, too long battling wars against ourselves, too long tugging and pulling at every inch of skin. It's time to stop.

Body, I'm sorry.

I'm sorry for all the words I spat, the self-hate I imposed, and the judgment I inflicted.

I'm sorry for the times I cut you, the burns I caused, the scarring that remains.

I'm sorry for the gorging and depriving, the pulling and tugging, the pinching and squishing.

I'm sorry for it all.

I'm sorry I hated you for not being what I needed. For using you for validation I sought, for giving you away without second guessing. I'm sorry for abusing you.

I'm sorry I thought you were never enough. For always demanding more, for pushing beyond limits out of spite for how you looked. I'm sorry for mistreating you.

I'm sorry I couldn't see your fight, the support you give me daily, whether I appreciate it or not. You have kept me alive and do so every day. I'm sorry I didn't see that.

Body, I am ready. I am ready to wave my white flag and surrender the fight. I am ready to heal, to mend all that was broken, and to find our peace again. I am tired of fighting; I don't want to do it anymore.

Body, I want to thank you. Thank you for never giving up and for showing me I was worth fighting for.

Thank you.

For every fight fought.

For every wound healed.

For every second chance given.

Thank you for fighting for me, thank you for loving me, thank you for healing me.

Unapologetically yours,

Lauren

10

See You in my Dreams

And just like that, she was gone
The world too harsh for her sweet soul,
The weight too heavy to carry anymore
The fight too long to bear.
Sweet dreams.

My hands shook as I hold the phone. I heard the words that sounded so wrong, the sentence I never expected to hear, the letters that didn't make sense, the voice I told myself wasn't real. I shook my head again and again as I argued, she was wrong. I fell quickly into a hole of denial…suppress, suppress, suppress. I felt my body convulse as the nothingness wouldn't come, the sensations increased and the awareness spiked. Please just let me go—let me run from this; let it not be true. I found my phone in my lap and forced my fingers to type the one question I needed to be answered—*Please tell me it isn't true.*

I stand lifeless as I watch her float. Her beautiful soul has left us, and yet I can still feel her love in the room. I stand back, afraid to step closer, watching as my loved ones sob at her bedside. I feel the pull, the desire to be near her, but I can't…not yet. I need space. I need time. I need words. I have so much to say, so much to apologise to her for, so much I need her to know. Words that I have to speak.

I stand frozen as I watch my family leave the room one by one, realising that the time is coming closer and closer, one I never thought we'd have. Our last goodbye. I ask for just one minute alone, just one last talk with her, one final word. I feel myself detach as my body moves, taking me away because it's far too painful here. I hover as I watch myself step closer, brushing her hair away from her face as a single curls fall. And the moment I feel her hair, the tears begin to fall. The all-too-familiar touch of her curls brings me undone. Would I really never do her hair again? Never hear her laugh? Never feel her hand? Never hold her close? Would I really never again…?

I close my eyes and allow the tears to fall, fast. I sob out the words I have to say. *I'm sorry. I'm sorry. I'm sorry.* I wanted so badly to heal her, to hold her hand through it all, to fight her fight with her. Side by side we could do this. But I didn't know how bad she got, I didn't know how lost or tired she had grown. I wish I knew.

I make a promise, then and there. I promised to never again do myself harm. Never again would I fall down the path we took. I swore I would fight this fight for us both, I would find the light and face the dark, and I would do this for us. I would be the voice, say the words we both needed to say, the help we both sought to find, the clarity we both wished to discover.

I sob every last word I need to say, say I love you, and walk away before I can never let go, fighting the desire to crumble. *Goodbye, sweet girl, I will see you in my dreams soon.*

In 2015, I lost my little cousin to suicide. She was battling a war I knew all too well, and one I couldn't save her from—none of us could. I thought up until that moment that I had my turning point already, the moment I was reborn and changed my life for the better. But deep down, I knew that wasn't the case anymore. I was still relapsing, still lost, still fighting a solo war against myself. And then I lost her, and everything changed.

Losing a loved one to suicide sucks. There's no other way to describe it. It's the creation of so many unanswered questions. It's dark and painful and all-consuming. It's destructive, heartbreaking, and gut-wrenching. It has the power to stop time while in the exact same moment evoke a desire to move ahead.

It divides families and unites them. It brings waves of emotions and numbness. It forces a whirlwind of actions and nothingness. It is harsh, confusing, and horrific—but it is life-changing.

Through losing a loved one to suicide, my life changed—our lives changed—and I found myself.

This became the moment my life changed forever. What people often see as a selfish act is a selfless one—she took her life and, in turn, gave us all our own. Because when something like that happens—when a life is taken so young—you have to change. You are forced to see things differently, and there is no way to continue on as you were before. And we are all forever changed.

I made a promise that day and I have kept it ever since. I promised myself that I would find my purpose in the world, that I would make something of myself, and that I would devote my life to bettering who I was which would then help those around me. There were no more excuses for me; it was time to change.

We all have a past; we all have a story, but no matter how dark that story is, I can promise you that you have a purpose in this world, and my hope is you see that. Because life is to unexpected to waste.

Unapologetically yours,

Lauren

11

Losing Love, Learning, and Loneliness

My heart feels heavy
Heavy and alone
My head confused
Confused and lost
My body weak
Weak and irrelevant
I've lost you, and I don't know what's left

I've done it again. I've lost him. I could see it coming, I could feel the push, I knew what I was doing. So why did I do it? Why did I push him over the edge?

I feel the weight of my loneliness crushing me. The realisation that there is nothing to stop it, nothing to soften the blow, nothing to suppress the emotions that are bubbling free. For the first time, I am forced to sit and feel the enormity of the emotions within and see them for what they are—to feel their release and face my truths.

My natural instinct to run and hide beneath the covers of self-destruction again. But I can't do it this time. I can't. I promised I was done, so what else do I have to do except face the waves before me and stand, openly, as they wash over time and time again.

And sometimes the weight of the loneliness sits so heavy on my chest that I struggle to find the release I need to set it free. It sits heavy and hard on my heart; it feels like it could consume me at any moment if I let it, taking me into the depths of the dark corners of my mind I try to avoid.

I run from it, push it back, down where it belongs but it seeps up, and through waves of loneliness rushing from my eyes, it escapes, unable to be contained for a moment longer. I crumble under the weight of the release as I feel it wash over me.

I close my eyes and let it come, let it take me, let it be.

I close my eyes and there you are. I feel your arms around me holding me close, protecting me from the demons I can't avoid. I close my eyes and I see you, your smile, the way you would look at me. I close my eyes and you are there. Even if only for a moment.

Because my mind knows…she knows you are gone. She knows loneliness shows what I had, that the love is still real, but just like the waves of loneliness, it, too, will pass.

But for now I let it come. I let the weight of the loss of you stay because it's a part of me, too, and I'll always have that part of you.

I allow my heart to rip open. My words, my fears, and my doubts fall onto friends' ears. I allow my floodgates to open sending tears trembling through my body. I allow the words to escape; things I never knew I felt run free into the world before me. I allowed myself to feel.

And under the weight of it all, under the waves of the emotions, the letting go of all I held deeply, I feel a release. Tears I restrained for years were free, the anger I never showed was gone, and the hurt I was afraid to admit ran wild. I felt open, at times empty, but above all…free.

Unapologetically yours,

Lauren

12

You Were a Love

I was afraid
Afraid of loving you
Afraid of you loving me
Afraid of what that would mean

You were a love I'd never felt. One that made me feel worthy again. A love that motivated me to *be* better and *do* better. A love that inspired me and showed me the light in my life I was too blind to see. A love that felt powerful enough to erase past heartbreak and heal my hope again. A love I didn't expect, but one that showed up when I wasn't looking. You were a love that healed.

You were a love full of lessons. A love that taught me things, challenged me, pushed me, and tested me. A love built on questions, 'what if's and 'why not's. A love that exposed me to sides of myself I didn't know lived, that guided me to find worth I didn't know I had. You were a love that taught.

You were a love that confused me. Left me contemplating my own thoughts and beliefs. The kind of love that forces you to feel, to stand in its true, raw beauty and wade through the emotions. A love that felt so purposeful yet so conflicting. A love that evolved.

You were a love that served me. The kind that you know will change you forever. The kind that leaves you completely different than what you once were. A love that never holds regret, for no matter how it ended, it served a beautiful and necessary purpose for the moment. A love that ended.

You were a love that left. A love that evaporated. A love that hurt.

And when you did leave, all that was left were the waves of confusion. The love that challenged and tested and pushed me was gone, and all that was left was me. I was left to stand raw and exposed in the harsh reality of the emotions swimming beneath me. Feeling them wash over me again and again with no lifeguard in sight.

But this time I didn't struggle; for once I didn't fight them, I surrendered. I allowed the waves to take me out to sea. I let myself cry, sob tears so heavy and long that my body ached under their weight. I allowed myself to scream, to throw, to punch, to curse your name, to feel the fire within my being and allow it to bubble free. I encouraged myself to release the regret, the guilt, and the 'what if's, setting them free to the ears of friends and loved ones. I let myself feel. *Truly* feel.

It was hard, losing you. It was. My body missed yours. It craved your skin's sweet kiss and the comfort during the night. My heart felt heavy, alone, and abandoned. I wasn't sure how to move on. Part of me wondered if I ever will completely let go. All of my previous beliefs and fears surfaced, but they rose for a reason. They showed me, reminded me again, that in life things come and go—nothing is forever, and the more I can learn to ride the waves of emotion, to see them for the benefit they bring, the better life I can lead.

Over time I have realised that I lost you but I gained myself. Without losing you, I wouldn't have found the woman before me today...and I'm actually okay with that.

If I hadn't lost you, I wouldn't have forced myself to feel, to encourage the emotions I once ran from to surface, or to feel the weight of tears or bursting energy of anger. I wouldn't have shown myself it is okay to feel, to stand true in the thoughts of my mind. I wouldn't have detached from the stories I tell of my feelings and just waved goodbye and set them free. If I hadn't lost you, I wouldn't have felt.

If I hadn't lost you, I wouldn't have the courage to stand in my voice and ask for what I want. I would have kept playing small and ignoring my inner self begging to be set free. I would have continued to send myself crazy, avoiding the voice I knew needed to be shared. I wouldn't have been forced to stand on my own again and embrace the fear of this, turning it into courage and confidence. If I hadn't lost you, I wouldn't have spoken.

If I hadn't lost you, I wouldn't be so aware. Going through heartbreak and feeling emotions I once ignored forced me to be aware of what happens in my mind. I wouldn't have seen the power of this or understood the potential outcomes. I wouldn't choose to see my every day with awareness and curiosity as I do now. I wouldn't understand myself the way I do now. If I hadn't lost you, I wouldn't understand.

Without losing you, I wouldn't be me. I have never felt more in touch with my true self than I do standing today. If I hadn't lost you, I wouldn't have space and time to learn about myself, to delve deeper into the crevices of my likes, dislikes, my soul. I wouldn't have the self-worth to comfortably invest in who I am and know I am worthy of the space and time. If I hadn't lost you, I wouldn't be me.

You were a love I needed, a love that healed, a love that truly served. A love that I will always hold dearly. But losing you, I am grateful for. I am okay with it. I needed it. Losing you gave me *me*, and that was a beautiful gift to be given.

Unapologetically yours,

Lauren

13

You Aren't Weak By Letting Him

I surrender to my softer side
Feeling her swoon in
Feeling the courage this takes
Seeing the strength within

I thought I was being strong…

I thought standing on my own two feet was strong.

I thought not needing a man—or anyone—was strong.

I thought declaring how independent I was was strong.

I thought faking smiles and refusing comfort was strong.

I thought being masculine was strong.

I was a strong woman. I identified with that 'Miss Independent,' and I paraded around with that label as my badge of honour. I knew who I was, what I needed, and what I could do, and no one would ever take this from me. I held the space for myself. I was strong.

I had been burnt before, and without a man, able to rebuild. I knew what needy felt like, and I shied away from its rising again. I knew what I didn't want to be, so I ran, attracting the opposite.

And when I had him, I made sure he knew that. I made sure it was clear: I was strong. I pushed and resented. I shuddered and squirmed. I refused and avoided. His masculinity I stole. I wore it on my own. I held the energy of us both—I needed that because I was strong enough without him.

Except…I wasn't strong.

Being a strong woman is to know I can do it alone but I'd like him to help. To know I don't need him, I want him.

Being a strong woman is to not need to declare it constantly. To not take his power away to ignite my own. To not feel inferior when he helps.

Being a strong woman is to be vulnerable enough to admit I'm not always strong.

I was avoiding, suppressing, and hiding. I was running from a weakness and a fear so big I couldn't stand to feel the weight of it grow anymore.

I can see now that I was weak. I was hiding behind a mask I had worn for too long—one of masculinity that didn't quite fit. I was withholding his power for unconscious lack of my own. I was holding space for the both of us, and there was no room for him left. I knew I needed him, I knew I needed help, I knew I wanted him, but I was too weak to show it. I was sure that showing him was a weakness; allowing him to be a man was weakness.

So I pushed. I didn't want to feel inferior, I didn't want to feel nurtured, and I didn't want to feel looked after.

I would cringe under his loving touch, reminding him, again and again, I didn't need him. Pushing further and further away.

All he wanted was to be a man, to stand in the power that was rightfully his.

And I can see now that letting him be that is strength.

Letting a man be a man takes strength.

It takes strength to admit you want his help.

It takes strength to feel comfortable with showing him you need him.

It takes strength to be able to stand by him without tearing him down.

To all the strong women out there: this is for you; we can do it alone.

We can. We don't need a man. We don't need admiration. We don't need his help.

We don't need someone to save us.

We don't need someone to comfort us.

We don't need someone to support us.

But life can be pretty beautiful when you let him.

We can be strong, but so can they.

We can embrace our own strength, our own power, our own light and stand together in the power of us both.

We can be hard and soft, intertwined together.

We can compliment and build together.

We can give and take and evolve together.

We can share the space, the masks, and the roles.

We can be strong and let him be, too.

Let him help. Let him be right sometimes (even if he's wrong). Let him not ask for directions or change the light bulb for you. Let him open doors and hold you when you hurt. Let him show you how he fixes things; let him tell you all about things he truthfully may know nothing about. Just let him.

If you find yourself gripping onto your masks with intention of never letting go, I beg you to ask yourself why.

Because there is space on both sides of us, of both of us, in this world.

It may be that we have been burnt before, but I promise it will be okay.

You're a strong woman, and even if you are burnt again, you'll rise from the ashes like you always do.

But for now, please let him help.

Unapologetically yours,

Lauren

PART 2

Evolve

And like a sunflower rising from the dirt
I will sprout
I will grow
I will evolve

14

I Don't Forgive You, I Thank You

I forgive you feels wrong
Like an invisible contract
I can destroy at any time
Words I can take back
Love I can avoid
Acceptance never sought

I said I forgave you. But what I didn't say was it came with clauses. I forgave you until you hurt me again. I forgave you until you failed me. I forgave you until you let me down. I forgave you until you proved me right…because what I didn't say was I forgave you with the deep belief you would never change and I expected you to fail.

My forgiveness was bullshit, a mask I hid behind to protect myself. Forgiveness was safe; it was quiet, kind, and soft. It said I was a good person and gave me comfort and praise. I was a good person for forgiving you, and that praise felt wonderful. But it was all fake.

Because I knew, *I knew* I wouldn't let it go; in my mind, you would forever be to blame. I knew my motives, the comfort I was seeking, the pride I needed. I knew what I was doing, so I forgave you.

But I don't.

I don't forgive you.

Because I don't need to.

I don't need to forgive you for what you did.

I don't need to forgive you for what you said.

I don't need to forgive you for the hurt you brought.

I don't need to forgive you at all.

Because no matter how destructive it felt, no matter how broken I became, no matter how painful it was…it was exactly what I needed.

Everything that happened has built my life to date. It was all for a purpose greater than us both. And no matter how wrong that feels to say, I know how right it is. I don't forgive you, but I do thank you.

And my gratitude doesn't come with clauses. It isn't conditional, it isn't fluctuating, it isn't seeking—it just is.

My gratitude is real. It's messy and uncomfortable, it's confronting and vulnerable, it's exposing and clear. It stripped me bare and left me standing naked with my truths, the truth that I only forgave you for me.

So I don't forgive you, but I don't need to. I need to thank you.

Thank you for all of it.

For the years of ups and downs, for the times of neglect, for the moments of vacancy, for the struggles, for the fights, for the hurt. Thank you for leaving, for ignoring, for straying. Thank you for loving, for returning, for trying. Thank you for it all.

It's taken some time, but I see the value in you, in me, and in us now.

So thank you, Mum.

Unapologetically yours,

Lauren

15

Some Days are Just Shit, so Let Them Be

It's the forced smiles,
The fake laughs
The hidden tears

I force a smile and hide my tears, telling myself I am okay. I hide the tissues and wipe my makeup, telling myself I am okay. I avoid their questions and fabricate answers, telling myself I am okay. But I'm not okay. Inside I am falling apart.

It's the fake smiles and forced laughs. It's the guilt-ridden messages and hidden reactions. It's the smug superiority and jaded texts. It's crap and it needs to stop.

It's the, "Everything's great!" when you're avoiding tears. It's the 'look on the bright side' when darkness is needed. It's the 'I should be grateful' when pity is serving. It's crap and it needs to stop.

It's the self-judgment, the guilty words, the avoidance, the discomfort, the ignorance. It's crap and it needs to stop.

In a world where there are always positives and negatives, highs and lows, it is suffocating to be surrounded by the constant push of positivity. No, I don't want to think of three things I'm grateful for when I've just lost a loved one. No, I don't want to look on the bright side when I've just experienced heartbreak. No, I don't want to smile when I need to release some tears. I don't want to be positive every moment of the day because I'm human and that is exhausting.

Life isn't always rainbows.

It isn't always happy endings.

A smile doesn't fix everything.

And everything we suppress needs to be expressed.

Sorry to burst your positivity bubble, but it needs to stop.

The truth is that some days do suck.

There is heartache,

misfortune,

pain,

loss;

these are all real parts of life.

And by suffocating under the weight of positive affirmations, we are not serving anyone—we are struggling to breathe.

Some days we just want to cry, and we need that. Through tears, we can release what we may otherwise fester in our hearts. So please, let us cry.

Some days we just want to complain, and we need that. Through complaining, we can vent and release the constant cycle of thoughts we are trapped in our minds. So please, let us complain.

Some days we just want to be angry, and we need that. Through anger, we release emotions that otherwise can grow into something deeper and harder to release. So please, let us rage.

Some days we just feel off, and we need that. Through allowing ourselves to go with whatever emotion rises we accept both highs and lows in life. So please, let us feel.

We don't need a guilt trip when we are feeling crummy already, we don't need a forced smile when we are feeling fake already, and we don't need yet another reminder of how lucky we are when we are feeling selfish already. Feelings are hard enough; don't add a side of guilt with our dish.

There is too much pressure in the world to always be a certain way, let's not add positivity to the mix.

I'm not a negative person, nor am I a positive one—I just am a human with two sides, plenty of emotions, and tired of being pressed for positivity.

So it's crap. Cut the positive chase and let us just be.

Unapologetically yours,

Lauren

16

There are Always Two Sides

And we walk around in a world of duality
There is no pain without pleasure
No success without failure
No positive without negative

My mind feels full. I wake with the pressure of what feels like a thousand thoughts pressing down hard on my forehead. My jaw clenched and teeth shut, I'm holding a thousand words captive. All of which I don't know what letters they hold.

And just like that, my old ways tug. Thoughts begin and excuses rise. Withdrawing is easier than facing the discomfort today. I feel the old me waving her arms, seducing me in, back to rescue her once again. But I know as soon as I swim too close and I am near her grips, she will hold on and make me her life raft once again. I know her seductive dance enough to know I might not win.

But the dynamic within me feels new today, different. I feel torn, somehow in the grey-faded middle between who I was and who I am becoming. Hovering in limbo waiting to make the choice, to decide who to be right now. Confusion rises as I realise that in the midst of my confusion is my clarity—this is my test. I can make excuses, allow discomfort to swallow me whole and forcing me to retreat. Or I can rise, step into the discomfort yet choose to see it for what it is, to turn inward to seek more, to allow myself to just be and whatever wave rises, to catch it open heartedly.

I choose to ride the wave, I welcome the tears of discomfort, the heaviness in my heart, the sadness in my body. I know it isn't here to stay. I choose to not to suppress it or force a positive outlook. Instead, I choose to slow down, to wade through the things that rise and to give them space. To put *me* first, and to listen to what I need in this moment. I give space to this side of me, for it is a part of me, too.

I am not one side; I am not only happiness, joy, or kindness. I am fear, sadness, and anger, too. I choose to see that today. To not force a side of me away that is real, a side of me I need.

So today, I choose to move slow, to allow my body to feel the weight of the sadness in my heart and give space to the fears within me. I choose to be curious but not judgmental about what comes up, to be aware of how I feel. Today I choose to be whatever I am right now. No forced smiles, no, "I'm okay"s, no side of optimism attached. Today I just am.

But it hasn't always been this way. I would once fight back, rebelling against my inner introvert, demanding a positive ray of sunshine. Every. Single. Day. And it was exhausting.

I would force myself to push beyond the brink of warning signs and red flashing lights until I would crumble under the weight of a thousand fake smiles. The load was too heavy to carry and the result was a silent, sobbing, confused, lost me.

The alternative was admitting that sometimes I needed to let my inner introvert out and wade through the uncomfortable thoughts which were too often too boring and too judged—by me. I thought that was a sulking side of me, a weak version I didn't wish to visit often. But looking back, she was a side who needed space sometimes, too.

The world of positivity, affirmations, 'seeing the bright side,' and, at times, overbearing optimism—has a place. We all need a cup of rainbows sometimes. *Sometimes* being the key word. We cannot walk around filled with positive words, fake smiles plastered on our suppressing faces every day. Nor are we supposed to. Yet in a world where the positivity is captivating, consuming, and at times very confusing, it is difficult to switch off from this.

When I began my journey to recovery, I thought this was the way. I saw the positive community as a stepping stone to recovery and thought through combining forces and adopting some of the very helpful (but again 'time and place required') tips, I would live a happy, healthy life. Unfortunately, I very quickly crumbled under the weight of all the positive affirmations.

Questions arose like, "Why am I not happy every day?" "Why does saying 'I am' over and over again feeling more fake and frustrating?" "Why is it becoming more exhausting the more days I spend trying to convince myself I am happy when I just feel, well…crummy?"

I had transitioned from a deep place of depression and despair to a world of positivity quite quickly. I had become a yo-yo of emotions and I was on the rise, and a quick rise it was. But like everything that rises, I needed to fall sometimes, too. By fighting against the laws of gravity, I was fighting against myself. And I was exhausted. I was tired of cycles, I was tired of extreme highs and lows, and I just wanted balance.

I needed to embrace the highs and the lows. The good days and the bad. The positive and the negative. Because both were a very real side of me; both were what made me up to be me. And both needed to have their own space.

So I stopped fighting the low days. Because like the girl before, I still wake up some days with a migraine of mental chatter, a clenched jaw, and a thousand words I can't make out how to say. It doesn't pass; there is no magic day where we wake up with them gone, but everything we suppress has to be expressed at some point. The sooner we see that, the sooner we see the benefit they bring—the purpose they serve—and the better life we can live.

You can't expect every day to feel great. Having a down day doesn't mean you're depressed, or boring, or a 'drag to be around.' It means you're human.

Give yourself a break and allow all sides of you space, too.

Unapologetically yours,

Lauren

17

Uncovering Solutions, Facing Truths, and Admitting Lies

I was that girl. The girl who would hide behind her statements of gratitude, force smiles, and pretend she was an optimist all the time. I would face the world with a shield of positivity, hiding from the harsh reality of my truth. My truth was that under it all, under the fake smiles and, "Everything is great," I was a mess.

I was that girl. The girl who fought back time and time again. To the world, I was resilient; I had overcome hardship. To the world, I was a survivor. And I thought I was one, too. But under it all, under the 'I can overcome anything' exterior, I was a mess.

I was that girl. The girl who shared uplifting quotes, who wrote positive captions and painted the world with bright colours. The colours to hide the deep, dark depths I saw in my life, to camouflage the internal pain I was feeling. To the world, I was inspiring, but inside, I was a mess.

I lived my life how I thought I 'should' live. I stood proudly under the recognition of being a survivor, the badge of honour I wore daily. But something didn't quite feel right. The badge was too big to bear, and at the end of every day, after wiping off my fake smiles and shielded reality—I crumbled. I couldn't see at the time that I was suffocating. I was suffocating in a world I had created for myself, one where I had to be happy, grateful, and positive. I had to show that I had overcome mental illness, self-harm, and all the other demons of my past. I had to show others I was okay, life was good, and everything was fine. I had to.

I thought by putting on the façade, showing the final edits, I was doing this. I told the world I was vulnerable, sharing every secret I kept. But what I failed to see was I was hiding. I was hiding behind the comfortable truths—the facts of my past. But how I felt now? The battles I hadn't won? I couldn't share them. I couldn't show the world that side of me. So I hid it.

I felt so disconnected from the voice I was sharing, the words I would post, the smiles I would force. I knew they weren't mine, and the falsity of it all created a further gap between who I was and who I thought I should be. I was living two lives and I was suffocating.

I now see that by hiding what was under the surface, I was falling captive to the façade I had created. I struggled to find my purpose because I was drowning under the fake smiles and forced affirmations. I struggled to be—to just be who I was—because I was always diminishing half of me, forcing the 'negative' side of Lauren away. I was showing up, with half of me, expecting a full outcome. I failed to see that by sharing all of me, by showing the lows as well as the highs, I would empower others with what I had to say, and I would truly be vulnerable and real with the people around me.

After all, no one wants to be told to smile when everything in their life is turning to crap, and in a way, I was doing exactly that.

I can see now that forcing one side of me, of us all, and suppressing another will never work. We live in a dualistic world. We know we can't have light without darkness, hot without cold, highs tides without low tides—so why do we think we are any different?

With every forced positive will come an equal negative. Think of how guilty you feel, how much you berate yourself when you are TRYING to be happy but you just don't feel it.

It just doesn't work.

I may not have always been as authentic as I hoped, or shared the thoughts behind my words, but I do now.

I am tired of the positivity trend and seeing people berate themselves time and time again when things don't work. Enough is enough.

So I will stand in my discomfort, be the honest voice I declare to be, and share the lows and the highs because they are all a part of life.

I encourage you to find your truth, too and stand boldly in the unknown. Share your voice—the voice that is truly yours. There is power in honesty. Embrace it—all of it.

Unapologetically yours,

Lauren

18

It's All Up to You

It begins and ends
With us.
One decision
One choice
One shift
Is all it takes…

We hold the ability to change not only our minds but our lives. We do. How empowering is that? We are the CEOs of our own lives; it is all up to us. The moment I realised this—the moment I saw the responsibility I had in my life, the leading role I played—was the moment everything changed. I shifted. I embraced. I evolved. I was aware of the impact I had within my world, and for me, this was empowering.

But with the empowerment also came...discomfort. I become uncomfortably aware that this not only meant I had to step up and take control, but I could no longer play the victim. And for me? This was petrifying. I knew how to be a victim; victim-hood was safe, a role I knew all too well. And letting go of this? Of all I knew? Of the comfort I sought? Terrifying.

I could no longer hide behind blame. My life was now solely in my control. No more justifications, no more labels, no more excuses—if I wanted a new life, it was up to me to build it. And the harsh reality of that was a wake-up call I needed.

This doesn't mean I immediately fell into a new life, letting go of my old mindset and releasing all I once was; it isn't that easy. I still have moments where I would rather hide behind excuses and blame everyone for my life's turmoils, and I am sure I will have many of those moments to come. But just like riding a bike, now I know what I do—I can never unlearn it. I will always have the knowledge that my life is up to me.

We know we can't change other people, only ourselves. So does it not make sense to take ownership of our lives and change whatever it is we aren't happy about? By doing the work on yourself, by taking stock of your own life and your own emotions, you, in turn, allow others to change AND you change how you perceive them. But again, you have to do the work.

Or don't. The decision is yours.

You can either choose to complain that your life is miserable and everyone around you is terrible, OR you can do something about the life you have in front of you and create the life of your dreams. I don't care how cliché that is, there are no limits in life—only the ones we create. Yes, we, see the common theme here? It is all up to us.

But be prepared: any changes you make in life won't be easy; they never are. Something I have learnt, that I think we all need to realise, is that there will always be this internal conflict whenever we are in the midst of change or in the process of growth. There is no growth without first facing a challenge, and this forces us to turn inwards again and see that we hold the power. It all comes back to us. When faced with a conflict we can either decide to continue through discomfort or allow the discomfort to take over and shrink back into who we once were. The decision is ultimately ours.

Either way, life goes on, but how our lives are impacted is up to us.

It all comes back to us.

And that can either be your empowerment or your undoing.

The choice is ultimately yours.

Unapologetically yours,

Lauren

19

You Aren't Broken

For so many years I told myself
I was broken
I was used
I was less than
I can finally see…
none of us are

You don't need to be fixed.

You aren't broken.

You aren't completed f&*ked up.

You have just been told you are, made to feel you are and believed you are.

Well, I am here to tell you that you're not.

None of us are.

The parts of you that you feel have left you broken have been the exact parts you needed to reach the space you are in now. Let that sink in—the parts of you that you feel are broken are the parts you needed to be in the place you are now. And that is exactly where you need to be.

Does that mean it's been easy? No.

Does that make it all okay? No.

Does that take away from your struggle? No.

All of the discomfort you have felt has been real, but it has been necessary.

We aren't readily taught this, but to reach anything we seek to achieve in life, to make any forward progress, to live each day and in turn grow—we have to face discomfort. Challenges will always be there. I'm sorry, but it's true. We can't change the facts, but we can change how we perceive them. Because whilst I'm sorry to burst your fantasy of a smooth-sailing life, I'm not sorry that discomfort exists. Through overcoming adversity not only do we grow and become stronger but we also become clearer on who we are and why we are here.

So while you may think you are broken because you continue to face hardship after hardship, or you feel you need fixing because you continue to f&*k up relationship after relationship, I'm sorry, but you aren't broken—that's just life.

The sooner we realise none of us are broken and stop labeling ourselves and disempowering ourselves by saying daily how broken we are, the sooner we can start fulfilling the life we are here to live.

It takes courage to face the truth of this. And I know you have the courage in you to do this.

Stop hiding behind the label of 'broken' and face the discomfort you are coming up against

Stop chasing a positive outlook and acknowledge the challenges your facing.

Stop avoiding the pain and step into discomfort.

Realise everything in your life is serving a purpose and start living your life—because you deserve that.

Unapologetically yours,

Lauren

20

I Just Am

And with tears streaming down my face
I close my eyes and smile
Knowing, finally knowing
I just am.

I don't know when it happened. I don't know how. But it did. I realised, I finally saw, I don't need to be enough—I just need to be me. Right now, as I am. I matter. I am important, so very important, and I cry, I sob as I realise that everything I went through all makes sense now. I am—we all are perfectly where we need to be.

I finally reached a space of knowing, truly knowing, that I don't have to be anything, I just have to be who I am. I will, and still do, falter. I crumble and at times feel less than, I question my journey, doubt myself, feel insecure—it all still happens, but I know in my core, that I am exactly where I need to be. I know now that by just being alive, by just being, that I am living my purpose.

And it brings tears to my eyes to admit it because for so long I felt I wasn't.

For so long I was searching for justification, proof, and confirmation that I was enough, that I was something. I needed it, I craved it. I was constantly seeking someone, even something short-lived, to prove I was enough. My body would long for another to kiss me in the night and affirm I was worthy.

My heart would seek another soul to reassure all the doubts and affirm I was loveable.

My ears would beg, beg for the words, the constant *I love you*, to affirm I was wanted.

I was constantly seeking out approval, constantly seeking for the high that would follow external validation and the internal self-talk of 'I am enough'.

But what I failed to see was I was hiding, suppressing a side of me and setting myself up to constantly chase a peak I couldn't sustain. I am both enough and not enough in the same shell. I am not one side of the equation, I am not only light with no dark, I am not all 'good' with no 'bad'. I am all of this, both sides of the coin, I just am.

Whether I am enough or not enough doesn't matter. Because they are both in of the same. There are times I am enough and others I am not, and that is the beauty of life. We are both sides, and neither is more superior than the other. It is just our perception, the story being 'enough' tells, that shifts how we feel about them.

And for me, I was tired of the story that society and I had fed myself…that I needed to be enough. Because in some ways, I wasn't, for some people I wasn't—and that's totally okay; I don't need to be.

And whilst I will still crave, at times, the high from being told I am enough, I no longer will crumble without the support of them to pick me up. I will curiously question the visit and follow the breadcrumb trail they leave behind to find their sender. Because my emotions are messages of different content but with the same purpose—to allow me to be aware and curious about what they have to say.

Unapologetically yours,

Lauren

21

I am Beautifully Chaotic

Chaos:
We fight to overcome it
We fight to avoid it
We fight to eliminate it
But what if chaos is
us?

It's the creation of storms in the calm I thought to avoid, the desire for waves in times of smooth seas, the internal battles I tried to diffuse. It's the part of me I attempted to change.

When did chaos become something we run from? Like dry leaves to flames, we avoid?

When did a chaotic mind and heart become a downfall? A quality we suppress?

Why do we see chaos in a negative light as inherently 'bad', something to avoid?

When we break down what Chaos is, and define the word as below, it has a quality of beauty about it.

Chaos—complete disorder and confusion. The infinity of space or formless matter to have preceded the existence of the universe. In Greek mythology defined as the first thing to exist. "At first came Chaos."

Are we then not able to see that how we perceive something depends on the context in which we view it? The perception we have in that moment?

I am one who would create chaos in calm, thrive in disorder, and feel most at home in times of turmoil. I told myself for years this was a 'bad' thing, that I was keeping myself stuck in cycles, attracting discomfort because it felt familiar to me. I was fighting to avoid a part of me, a quality I shouldn't embrace. I was rebelling against my beautiful chaos, and in turn, attracting it.

What I failed to see was that running from the thing I thought I should avoid was dragging me to stand in the face of the fire again and again.

I am beautifully chaotic.

I thrive under disorder.

I grow within discomfort.

I embrace times of confusion.

This doesn't mean it feels comfortable or easy or enjoyable when times are tough, but it does mean that embracing this side of me allows me to see the purpose of all the events along the way. My mind is no longer a place I seek to avoid but instead, I marvel at the constant push and pull within. My heart is no longer heavy and a place of fear but instead, it is a beautiful vessel to carry all of my desires. My life is no longer full of running or wishing to conform but instead, it is a reflection of embracing all I am.

I am beautifully chaotic and so proud of it.

Unapologetically yours,

Lauren

PART 3

Empower

We cannot change others,
but by first changing ourselves
we can empower others
to do the same

22

Be a Curiosity Chaser with Me

The questions beneath the surface;
I feel the excitement bubble
As they realise
They are finally being set free

And then I realised, all of the years of asking why, of wanting to know what was wrong, why me, what caused me to feel so…broken—all the curiosity was leading to now. Because with my curiosity I was finally able to see that everything I needed was in me all along. I just needed to listen.

In life, I believe we need to approach our world with the mind of a toddler. You know the age where they ask *why* to everything? Such an inquisitive nature which we often shut down with, "Because I said so." But—seeing it as a frustration we don't want to face—what if instead we encouraged the questions and followed their curiosity with them? What if we embraced curiosity, as well, and ourselves asked why?

Have you ever found yourself noticing you reacted differently to others in certain situations? Reacting strongly to words said or actions taken? Feeling emotional without an incident occurring? Feeling like something just isn't right but not being sure what?

And when you do, what do you normally do?

If you're anything like I was, you brush it off. I would find an excuse like the weather, the time of year, or think "I'm just being sensitive" and brush off the nagging feeling in my stomach. It was easier to hide behind a self-diagnosis of my emotional responses than to figure out the cause.

Until finally, like everything we suppress, it would be expressed some time later, maybe months down the track, when I would emotionally crumble and fall apart without knowing why.

A cycle I grew tired of partaking in.

I had tried to be positive, I had tried therapy, I had tried medication, I had tried avoidance, acceptance, suppression—I had tried everything, and I was tired of it all. But through my tiredness came anger. I was angry I couldn't seek help, I was angry nothing worked, I was angry I felt so broken. And my anger brought curiosity—an openness to try ANYTHING because something had to give.

My curiosity became a beautiful vessel, carrying me to clarity I had sought for years, allowing me to try and fail, experiment with what would work for me. My curiosity became my love, my passion, my desire—I sought out to follow it and lean into it regularly.

It wasn't until I started asking myself the questions I once did—like, "Why do I feel this way?" "What's going on for me?" "Why isn't anyone else like this?"—that I was able to see the power of asking why. Because by asking the right questions, I got the answers I was seeking.

Once I channeled my desire to know more about myself and my life, I began to uncover embedded self-limiting beliefs I had for years, discover emotions that were ruling my life, and become more aware of what I needed to live my best life. I continued to realise that the more curious I was, the less judgemental I felt, the more aware I was, the better life I could lead. I began to feel in tune with who I was for the first time. All by asking myself questions I needed to know.

Now, whenever I react strongly to something, feel 'off' without knowing why, or respond to others in a way I wouldn't usually—I ask why. I allow my words to run freely from my mind to my journal, phone, whatever is nearby, and ask what is happening for *me*.

I believe the most valuable thing we can achieve in life is to understand ourselves. So I will embrace my inner questioning toddler and continue on the chase for curiosity because this is a journey; there is no end point, so I will remain curious and chase my inquisitive nature.

Unapologetically yours,

Lauren

23

Finding Purpose

I choose to see
All sides of my life
With a curious heart and eyes of awareness
I see how my life serves me
All of me...

...and when I look back I know that everything has been and will continue to be perfect. All of the turmoil, the heartbreak, the failures, the mistakes, the success, the love, the achievements—it is all perfect. Every perceived pain I faced served me to reach the space I'm in now. I am here to embrace my past, evolve as a human, and empower others to do the same.

I have reached a place where I can comfortably look back on my young life so far, the memories of my past, and say it was all perfect. At first, I squirmed under the weight of those words, screaming inside that my pain was not perfect; none of it was. I fought back, rebelling against the truth hidden behind those words, determined I was hard done by and wronged. I clung so tightly to the label of victim, to the idea my life happened TO me, not FOR me. I refused to see that everything up till now has served me. My pain, I thought, could never serve me.

Yet once I reached this place, once I acknowledged both sides of every perceived heartache I experienced, I was able to see with a clear mind and no emotional reactions that my past was exactly what I needed. Because without it—without *all* of it—I wouldn't be who I am today.

It's more than my past making me stronger, it's not solely about my resilience being built, it's about having the awareness and making the choice to see both sides of everything in life. By seeing how something both hinders and serves me, I can be grateful for it. I can allow it to be a stepping stone on the way but not IN the way of my life. It simply is a step—not good or bad, just a step.

For me, this was the most freeing realisation. No longer did I have to be trapped by my past, stuck in a cycle of victimhood, securing my future by tying the ropes tighter and tighter. I was internally free from this, and it's a feeling I hope everyone uncovers.

Life isn't here to be easy; we aren't here to just be happy, and those who think we are unfortunately will keep repeating the same cycle they are currently in. Because by chasing a one-sided world, we will attract more and more of what we are avoiding. By chasing an easy, happy life, we will continue to run into challenge, depression, and frustration. We cannot have one without the other. So whilst life isn't here to be easy, it is here for us to grow. For when we stop growing...we die. Let go of the need to be happy and seek growth.

Everything you have endured up to now was perfect. I know how wrong that feels to read, to say, or to hear, but it's true. It was all necessary to get you to the point you are at right now. I know how horrific some lives have been, I do, but would everyone be the people they are today without them? And how awful would it be to not have those people be who they are?

Think of your loved ones, the people you unconditionally love around you and consider this. If they weren't the people they are today, if they hadn't gone through all of the adversity they have, if they hadn't overcome the battles they have fought—would they be the same person?

It sounds heartless, but our pain is exactly what we needed at the time.

We all have a purpose in this world, and often this is found through our pain.

I want to encourage you to reflect on your life so far, to see the heartache you have felt, and ask yourself if you would truthfully be the woman or man you are today without it.

Unapologetically yours,

Lauren

24

My Final Letter

My hope is through my letters, you found something you needed. Even a single sentence that stirred a deeper questioning within. We are all so capable, so valuable, and so purposeful in our lives. No matter the past you have endured or the present you face, I need you to know, I promise you this—you are here for greatness.

In every dark moment, know there is always a light.

In every heartache, know there is love.

In every wrong turn, there is always an alternate route.

You are never too late, too far gone, too stuck.

You can always change your life.

I'll be the honest voice to help you along, but the work, the change, the decision to break free? It comes down to you.

You have to choose to change your life.

Don't you think you owe yourself at least that?

Unapologetically yours,

Lauren

About the Author

Lauren Darlington is a 23-year-old girl who is chasing her curiosity to learn more about herself and the world around her. She is here to empower others to break free from their limits and step into their own curiosity as she has learnt by asking the right questions to find the answers we seek.

She aims to be an honest voice to the world because we have enough filters to hide behind as it is.

Find Lauren on Instagram @lllaureenn, on Facebook at facebook.com/llaurendarlington, or on her website, LettersfromLauren.net.

YOU MIGHT ALSO LIKE:

Your Soul is a River
by Nikita Gill

You Are Enough
by Becca Martin

Bloodline
by Ari Eastman

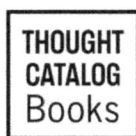

THOUGHT
CATALOG
Books

THOUGHT CATALOG

IT'S A WEBSITE.

www.thoughtcatalog.com

SOCIAL

facebook.com/thoughtcatalog
twitter.com/thoughtcatalog
tumblr.com/thoughtcatalog
instagram.com/thoughtcatalog

CORPORATE

www.thought.is

www.ingramcontent.com/pod-product-compliance
Lightning Source LLC
Chambersburg PA
CBHW031625040426
42452CB00007B/687